# EMOTIONAL INTELLIGENCE

*21 Powerful Strategies for Improving Your Social Skills and Increasing your EQ for Life and Work*

# TABLE OF CONTENTS

Introduction ............................................. 1

**Chapter 1: Understanding Emotional Intelligence** ........................................... 4

    How do you know you have good EQ? ........ 6

    When is emotional intelligence right and when is it wrong? .......................................... 8

    The elements of emotional intelligence ...... 10

    Characteristics of people with high or low emotional intelligence .................................. 15

**Chapter 2: The Role of Social Intelligence to Happiness in Life and Work** ..................................................... 21

    What is Social Intelligence? ....................... 23

    Why you need Social Intelligence .............. 24

The aspects of Social Intelligence .............. 26

The dimensions of social intelligence ........ 29

Characteristics of people high on Social Intelligence .................................................. 30

## Chapter 3: The Language of Emotional Intelligence ........................................ 36

Dimensions of Emotional Ability In The Context of Non Verbal Communication ..... 37

Why people fail to express emotions ......... 44

## Chapter 4: How to Master your Emotion and Improve Your EQ ......................... 48

The reasons behind the limiting emotions 49

Exercises to improve your emotional intelligence .................................................. 54

## Chapter 5: The Role of EQ in Effective Leadership ............................................. 64

The basis of effective leadership ................. 65

What happens when emotions of group members are not understood? .................... 66

Traits of an effective leader ......................... 68

Emotional Leadership Exercises ............... 69

## Chapter 6: 21 Powerful Strategies to Improve your EQ and Social Skills ...... 73

Why you need Social Skills ......................... 74

Social skills you need and how they help in achieving social success .............................. 76

Communicating Clearly ............................. 83

Mastering Emotions ................................... 86

Exercises to develop your social skills ....... 93

**Conclusion** .......................................... 100

**Bonus Content** .................................... 104

© Copyright 2019 by _____
All rights reserved.

The following eBook is reproduced below with the goal of providing information that is as accurate and reliable as possible. Regardless, purchasing this e-book can be seen as consent to the fact that both the publisher and the author of this book are in no way experts on the topics discussed within and that any recommendations or suggestions that are made herein are for entertainment purposes only. Professionals should be consulted as needed prior to undertaking any of the action endorsed herein.

This declaration is deemed fair and valid by both the American Bar Association and the Committee of Publishers Association and is legally binding throughout the United States.

Furthermore, the transmission, duplication, or reproduction of any of the following work including specific information will be considered an illegal act irrespective of if it is done electronically or in print. This extends to creating a secondary or tertiary copy of the work or a recorded copy and is only allowed with an express written consent from the Publisher. All additional rights reserved.

The information in the following pages is broadly considered a truthful and accurate account of facts. As such, any inattention, use, or misuse of the information in question by the reader will render any resulting actions solely under their purview. There are no scenarios in which the publisher or the original author of this work can be in any fashion deemed liable for any hardship or damages that may befall them after undertaking information described herein.

Additionally, the information in the following pages is intended only for informational purposes and should thus be thought of as universal. As befitting its nature, it is presented without assurance regarding its prolonged validity or interim quality. Trademarks that are mentioned are done without written consent and can in no way be considered an endorsement from the trademark holder.

# INTRODUCTION

This book contains 21 Powerful Strategies for Improving Your Social Skills and Increase your EQ for Life and Work. It presents a description of what Emotional Intelligence is and how acquiring the skills to enhance it will greatly change your social and work life.

Time was when most people consider mental or cognitive ability as the major contributor to an individual's success in life and at work. Success then was associated with a broad array of mental abilities, such as memory, reasoning, judgment, and abstract thought. As such, IQ was held as the standard of excellence for success in life until Daniel Goleman came up with his best-selling book on emotional intelligence.

Goleman's book popularized the concept of emotional intelligence and caught the attention of researchers, scientists, the public, and the media. But today, scientists claim a connection between emotional abilities and prosocial behavior, reduction of violence in schools, and its effective application in the workplace. Now, people from all professions incorporate emotional intelligence into their social and professional practices.

You can benefit from the use of emotional intelligence and achieve happiness in your personal, social, and professional life. This book shows you how to acquire the abilities to improve your emotional and social intelligence.

Thanks for downloading this book. I hope you enjoy it!

# CHAPTER 1

# UNDERSTANDING EMOTIONAL INTELLIGENCE

Imagine a situation where you receive a job offer, and you see it as a great opportunity in terms of salary, advancement, and location. But, you feel uneasy about resigning from your present job and moving on. Confronted with this situation, will you disregard your feeling and choose the logical path of accepting the job? Or, will you follow your feeling and disappoint your family?

Solving problems and making decisions entail thoughts and feelings, or you can say logic and intuition, both of which are part of what is referred to as emotional intelligence. You may have faced similar situations where you have to make wise decisions. Being able to understand your emotions and the emotions of others, you can use the knowledge to achieve success in life.

What is emotional intelligence?

Emotional intelligence is that ability which enables you, not only to recognize your emotions and that of the other people but to understand and control the emotions. Being able to control your emotions is valuable, especially in stressful moments.

Another way of looking at emotional intelligence is to view it as noncognitive – emotional and social – abilities, skills, and competencies that allow you to cope with environmental pressures and demands.

Emotional intelligence involves knowing what you feel when interacting with others, understanding how others feel, and using that knowledge to act constructively for your interest and that of the other people. It calls for your ability to empathize, to be resilient when confronted with difficulties, to control your impulses, and manage stress.

The end purpose of using emotional intelligence is to achieve prosocial behaviors. It can be used to come up with a win-win solution to a difficult situation where both end of the parties benefit. But, there is a dark side to emotional intelligence that you should be aware of in order to protect yourself.

## How do you know you have good EQ?

EQ is crucial to your success in life; therefore, developing the right EQ skills is crucial. You will know if you or the other person you are facing has the right EQ competencies:

- When you are aware of your feelings, recognize them when they occur, and be able to discriminate them.

- When you can handle your feelings, making them relevant to the current situation so you can respond accordingly.

- When you can motivate yourself, collect your feelings, and lead yourself toward a goal despite inertia, self-doubts, and impulsiveness.

- When you can recognize and empathize with the feelings of others and sync into their nonverbal and verbal cues.

- When you can handle interpersonal interactions, resolve conflicts and negotiate successfully.

There is, however, a dark side to emotional intelligence. By itself, emotional intelligence is morally neutral. One who has mastered emotional intelligence can use it to protect or promote the self. Or, the skills can be used to promote the self at the expense of others.

Studies have shown that people with high EQ can assess and control emotions to advance their own interests or achieve their personal goals. A report made by Dr. Martin Kilduff argues that EQ has a dark counterpart to the principles of EQ. Persons with high EQ use this ability to intimidate, spin, and manipulate individuals or groups to influence them and conform to one's will.

## When is emotional intelligence right and when is it wrong?

A person with high EQ abilities and competencies can misuse or abuse EQ by:

Strategically detecting emotion – the skill is used to analyze colleagues with regards their emotional state and pick up on nonverbal clues. The information they get will then be used for personal advantage.

Control display of emotions – persons high on EQ can hide their emotions, like a poker player. Or, they can express strong beliefs not held just to advance the self, at the expense of others.

Shape and stir the emotions of others - Persons high on EQ are adept at appearing sympathetic to another person, while silently shaping and stirring the other person's emotions. A master EQ performer can listen to your account of a story while the master performer puts emphasis on the negatives and disregards the positives. This is referred to as strategic empathizing which unbalances the other person, especially if the other person is viewed as a threat by the perpetrator.

While knowledge of the prosocial end of EQ can help you in several ways, it is prudent to be aware of its dark side. This knowledge can protect you from people who might abuse their EQ abilities.

# The elements of emotional intelligence

There are those who consider EQ to be more significant than the IQ in bringing about success in life and work. It is believed that success would depend on how well you read your own emotions, the emotions and cues – verbal and nonverbal - of others around you, and how you respond in appropriate ways. Otherwise, with the inability to read and interpret emotions, success will be far from your reach in life and at work.

A step towards good EQ is to understand its five categories:

### Self-awareness

This is an EQ competency which allows you to recognize your emotion as it occurs. Self-awareness is the key to emotional intelligence since all the other categories depend on recognizing, identifying, and understanding our emotions.

To develop self-awareness, you need to be attuned to your true feelings. If you are able to identify your feelings, you can manage and control them. Being self-aware involves emotional awareness where you recognize your feelings and its effects, accurate and objective self-assessment which allows you to examine your strengths and limits, and self-confidence, which means you are certain of your worth and capabilities.

**Self-regulation**

Once you have recognized and identified your feelings, you have to express, manage, and regulate these feelings appropriately. Self-regulation involves:

- Self-control to manage disruptive impulses and emotions

- Trustworthiness in adhering to a standard of integrity and honesty

- Conscientiousness – which means you claim responsibility for your actions and performance

- Adaptability – where you are able to handle change and are flexible

- Innovation – where you welcome and acknowledge new ideas and information.

**Self-motivation**

It has been shown that people high on EQ have high intrinsic motivation. They are driven by internal reasons rather than external rewards, such as fame, wealth, or respect. Achieving self-motivation involves:

- Achievement drive where you strive to improve performance or conform to a standard of excellence

- Commitment – where you align your goals with that of the group or organization

- Initiative – to be ready to act when you see an opportunity

- Optimism – where you persist with your goals despite setbacks and obstacles encountered.

**Empathy**

This is an ability which enables you to understand what the other person thinks, feels, and sees the condition from the other person's point of view. Empathy comes from within you, not forced, and allows you to be compassionate to the other's feelings. Empathy involves:

- Service orientation - a helping behavior where you anticipate, recognize, and meet the needs of others.

- Developing others – this involves sensing what others need, helping them develop, and boosting their abilities.

- Leveraging diversity – where you cultivate opportunities through diverse people.

- Political awareness – where you are able to read emotional currents and power relations within a group.

- Understanding others – where you discern what the others feel underneath their wants and needs.

**Social Skills**

Developing interpersonal skills is as good as experiencing success in your career and life. Social skills allow you to socially interact with people and navigate through social situations with success. The social skills you need are:

- Influence – apply persuasive tactics effectively

- Communication – sending and reading verbal and nonverbal cues effectively.

- Leadership – where you guide and inspire people.

- Change catalyst – where you initiate and manage change.

- Manage conflict – where you are able to understand, negotiate, and resolve disagreements.

- Build bonds – where you nurture instrumental relationships, inspiring cooperation within groups to achieve a goal.

- Collaboration and Cooperation – where you work with others to achieve shared goals.

## Characteristics of people with high or low emotional intelligence

According to Daniel Goleman, having a high IQ or being smart will not bring you success if you don't have emotional intelligence.

We can learn what effects having a high or a low emotional intelligence does to an individual by looking at some traits of people high on emotional intelligence. We can then compare these with people of low emotional intelligence.

People with high intelligence are:

- not afraid of change. They see change as a fact of life and are quick to adapt.

- aware of their strengths and weaknesses – where they excel, what to work on, what to learn, and the kind of environment that optimizes their abilities.

- comfortable relating with others and make the others feel special. They have the innate ability to understand what the others are going through.

- after quality, but accept that perfection is not real. They face difficulties, learn from mistakes, and move on.

- able to balance their personal and professional life. They keep their body fit and healthy and engage in interest aside from work.

- innately curious and possess a sense of wonder you would love to be with them. They are not judgmental, ask questions, look into possibilities, and open to new solutions.

- thankful for each new day, feel good living, and not bothered by critics or toxic people.

- highly focused. They have the ability to focus on the task on hand despite busy surroundings, interruptions, and distractions.

- guarded and wary, keeping boundaries with others, and know how to say "No", knowing that saying "Yes" all the time will only bring about stress.

- forgiving, no grudges, don't bark on past arguments, and quick to move on. Their outlook is positive and accepts the fact that people make mistakes. They don't waste time on anger and on things they can't change.

On the other hand, people with low emotional intelligence:

- cannot control their emotions.

- have no inkling about the feelings of others.

- unable to maintain good personal, social, and work relationships.

- think other people are overly sensitive.

- intolerant of other people's views.

- cannot handle emotionally-charged situations.

- pass mistakes on to others.

- often get into arguments.

- unable to regulate emotions and often display sudden emotional outbursts.

# CHAPTER 2

# THE ROLE OF SOCIAL INTELLIGENCE TO HAPPINESS IN LIFE AND WORK

The popularization of emotional intelligence led to researches in the biology and brain sciences. These studies reveal that people are "wired to connect" and that this connection, which appears even from infancy, has deep impact on people's relationships on all aspects of their lives. This need to connect roots from how we evolved as humans – people who can find themselves in a group tend to survive longer.

People connection is an emerging science which discovered that our brain is designed to make us sociable, naturally drawn to a brain-to-brain connection each time we engage with another person. The neural connection affects the brain, and consequently the body, of people in interaction.

Even the most mundane interactions with others act as brain regulators that prime our emotions. The effect may either be desirable or not. It follows that the stronger a person is connected to someone, the greater the emotional mutual force. While the brains are connected, feelings go through a roller coaster.

Social interactions act as modulators which continually reset key facets of our brain function as they manage our emotions. Relationships, therefore, mold our experiences, shaping us in small to profound ways. Social relationships that are nourishing, then, benefits us while toxic relationships destroy our bodies.

Social intelligence brings out the best in you and makes you keen on exploring your hidden potential. Understanding, therefore, social intelligence is necessary if you are to bring out your hidden potentials and make a success of your social life.

## What is Social Intelligence?

Where IQ is what you are born with, Social intelligence (SI) is learned. We learn SI through our experiences and interactions with people. We pick up SI through our successes and failures in social contexts. You may know of it as common sense, tact, or street smarts.

In general terms, social intelligence is indicated by your ability to "get along" with others. But, getting along is but a part of the definition. The other part is encouraging others to cooperate with you.

Social intelligence is often referred to as "people skills." It is an ability which encompasses your awareness of situations, social dynamics, what you know of interaction styles, how you interpret the stimuli presented by people you are interacting with, and strategies that would help you achieve your objectives in dealing with others.

Social intelligence, however, goes both ways. While you may be able to get others to cooperate with you, there is always that possibility that you can be swayed towards what others aim for in a social interaction. And, following Karl_Albrecht's classification of social behaviors, the effect of an interaction may either be "nourishing" or "toxic."

## Why you need Social Intelligence

People are innately social beings. This was so in early history and remains to be so today. Social intelligence is a prosocial behavior, which means how you understand and manage people to behave wisely in human relations.

If you are high on social intelligence, you have the nourishing behavior which makes people feel respected, valued, affirmed, encouraged, or competent. A person with a toxic behavior, on the other hand, tends to make people frustrated, angry, devalued, guilty, and inadequate.

Between the two types of social behavior, it is easy to see which behavior will bring you success. People with nourishing behavior are sought after by others, pulled by a "magnet" towards them.

On the opposite end, you have the toxic people who tend to alienate people. People tend to stay away from toxic persons, resulting to the isolation of that person.

It is possible, though, that toxic people are not aware of their behavior. They are so preoccupied with their own stresses that they are blind to the effects of their behavior on other people. They may need to go through radical personality changes to make them aware of how the others see them.

There is, however, hope for people who are low on social intelligence. Social intelligence is a learned ability and can, therefore, be cultivated and nurtured.

## The aspects of Social Intelligence

Making social intelligence a subset of emotional intelligence limits man's capacity for relationship and what transpires during an interaction. Further research on the concept of social intelligence went beyond this limitation.

The broad spectrum of social intelligence can be clustered into two categories: social awareness (being aware of others) and social facility (what is done about people awareness).

- Social awareness goes from primal empathy or the instantaneous awareness of the other's inner state, to empathic accuracy which makes us understand the other's thoughts and feelings, and lastly, to social cognition, getting the sense of a complicated social situation.

- Social facility involves how you present yourself to others, the influence and concern you exert or impress, and how you interact smoothly on the nonverbal level.

The two aspects complement each other. It is not enough to be aware of the other's inner state. You need to do something about your awareness of the inner state of the other person. You need to use what you sense of the inner state and of the complicated situation to allow for a smooth and effective interaction.

Bothe social awareness and social facility range from what is referred to as "low-road" and "high-road" capacities. A "low-road" lies underneath an individual's awareness and the effect is automatic and without effort. An example of a "low-road" effect is when you get fascinated by an attractive face.

In contrast, a "high-road" goes through the neural system and is, therefore, more methodical, going through an orderly process with conscious effort. Because you are fully aware, you have control over your inner life. This awareness is absent in the "low-road." For instance, when you think about your attraction to a face, you are taking the "high-road."

To be high on social intelligence, you need to embrace social awareness and social facility, as well as, the "low-road" and the "high-road." They serve as the key to human relationships and to social success.

# The dimensions of social intelligence

Social intelligence is a mix of skills and abilities. For instance, you need to have the ability to understand people and the skill to interact and communicate effectively with them.

For you to get along with others and get them to cooperate with you, it helps if you understand the five dimensions of social intelligence:

- Presence – this is how you present yourself to others. It is your outside image or your self-sense that is perceived by others, such as confidence, self-worth, or self-respect.

- Clarity – refers to how clearly you present yourself to others, the accuracy of the concepts you present, and how you effectively communicate ideas in order to persuade others.

- Awareness – refers to how you read social contexts and how these contexts impact behavior. From understanding the social contexts, you choose the appropriate behavioural strategy that will give you success.

- Authenticity – refers to the kind of behavior you perform which conveys a perception of honesty with one's self and of others .

- Empathy – refers to your ability to connect with others and encourage them to be "with" you rather than "against" you. This element includes your ability to appreciate the experiences and emotions of others.

## Characteristics of people high on Social Intelligence

People vary to the extent that they possess social intelligence. Various researches describe the characteristics of people high on social intelligence. One such report by Shaun Killian, an Australian educational psychologist came up with five characteristics of socially intelligent leaders, which can also be applied to one's social life:

1. Confidence in social situations – people high on SI present themselves with conviction and are comfortable with a social audience. These people are not self-conscious or shy. For them, the social situation is about the other people. They don't get affected by negative feedback.

2. Genuine interest in others – When in a social interaction, these people forget their own mental distractions and focus on the interest of others. This ability is known as "being in the moment" or "being fully present" which allows you to be truly responsive during conversations.

Responsiveness here refers not only on the cognitive level but on the "feeling" level –

reading the inner state of the other person in the context of the present situation.

A genuine interest in the other manifests itself even when you are alone. And, this caring show in simple and complex behaviors, like when you are on time for appointments, when you maintain eye contact with the person you are interacting with, when you anticipate the needs of others and offer them refreshments. Without a genuine interest in the other person, the situation is viewed as manipulation.

3. "Read" and respond to others – Being present in the situation is but part of a social interaction. You also need the ability to listen and be attentive to the other person. These people know how to "read" facial expressions, interpret messages conveyed through body language and tone. They can put these clues together to understand the inner state of the other person.

4. Express emotions and feelings clearly – Not all messages are conveyed verbally. Even stronger communication channels are non-verbal, such as body language, gestures, and tone of voice. And, non-verbal cues are contagious and goes both ways. What you see from the other affects you and what the other sees in you affects the person you are interacting with.

5. If you express authentic emotions and feelings, the other person will catch them. For instance, if your expressions exude interest and joy, the other person will be encouraged to interact with you.

6. Understanding social environments – This characteristic calls for a basic knowledge of people and of the social world applied to the context of the present social situation. This means understanding the different personalities of persons you are in contact with – they could be in your home, neighborhood, or in the workplace.

7. Knowledge of people will help you to encourage and motivate them, and help you deal with different personalities in different ways. And, you also need to know understand the norms and values of different individuals or groups you are with.

# CHAPTER 3

# THE LANGUAGE OF EMOTIONAL INTELLIGENCE

Each time we interact with another, we constantly give and receive nonverbal cues. These are powerful messages communicated without words, such as gestures, how fast or loud we talk, how we stand, the eye contact we make, and our facial expressions. Even your silence is a cue.

How we understand and make use of these signals determines how we express our feelings, manage the impressions we get, influence others, and form and define our relationships.

## Dimensions of Emotional Ability In The Context of Non Verbal Communication

People who communicate affectively are discerning and proficient in interpreting and using nonverbal communication to achieve their ends. For instance, they can accurately tell through observed facial expressions, if a person is sad, happy, angry or frustrated. A person's stand can also reveal that person's level of comfort and level of engagement. If your contact is too long, you appear aggressive; too short may convey hidden motivations.

Not all people are proficient in reading and interpreting nonverbal communication. Some are unable to perceive the intended messages or fail to appraise the meanings behind the nonverbal cues and use them as meaningful information.

Proficiency in nonverbal cues is the key to effective communication, which, in turn, depends on your ability to manage stress, perceive emotions, and understand the cues conveyed and received.

Emotional ability encompasses four branches or dimensions related to nonverbal communication:

**Perceiving Emotion**

This refers to the ability to identify and distinguish emotions in a given situation. This also includes identifying the source of the emotion, which could be yourself, the other person, or the situational transaction itself. Your first perceptions of the other person's emotions affect your capacities and thoughts, allowing you to manage your emotional response.

**Facilitating Emotion**

This refers to the ability to think, assess, and incorporate emotional information to be used as basis for decisions to achieve your goal. One who is knowledgeable in facilitating emotions incorporates the emotional information received in the present context with learned information from the past experiences to analyze their feelings and choose the best emotional responses. It is, therefore, important for you to identify which of the emotions you perceive in an interaction is useful for your purpose.

For instance, if you happen to be interacting with an angry person, instead of responding aggressively, a person skilled in emotional ability will choose the appropriate response that will moderate the tension.

Studies have shown that feelings and nonverbal communication can influence how emotions process thoughts and how differences in thoughts can affect one's understanding of emotions. Or, to put it simply, when people misunderstand their feelings, they are liable to make poor choices.

**Understanding Emotion**

Emotions change over time and situations. If you are to understand emotions, you need to be able to analyze complex emotions and predict how they may change. One who is proficient in reading emotions know that emotions could mix, blend, and change and that actions can have either short- or long-term consequences.

Unfortunately, many are poor in anticipating how one feels in the future. This is also referred to as affective misforecasting. When a person cannot predict the changing emotions, that person fails to see what makes for happiness and experience difficulty seeing beyond the filter of the present. The inability to understand emotion will be blinded by the current feelings and will be unable to make appropriate decisions in the future.

## Managing Emotion

This ability calls for the regulation of one's emotions and that of the others to achieve one's purpose. One who is skilled in managing emotions knows how to control emotions, avert impulsive reactions, and perform appropriate responses to a given social situation.

Emotions and emotional responses often are implicit and automatic. You need to prevent emotions, especially negative emotions, to spill from one concern to another unrelated concern.

## Communicating emotions effectively

There are three rules that define how we communicate our emotions effectively: the framing rule, feeling rule, and emotion work.

## Framing rule

This defines the emotional tone present in a situation. This rule depends on the culture of the persons in communication; it is, therefore, broad. It defines the topic, the time and context, and the specific situation. Here, the tone and atmosphere depends on the culture you are in. Examples are funerals are other somber events in Western culture.

**Feeling Rule**

This guides you to a proper emotion to feel in a particular situation. This rule reflects the values of a specific group or society and the roles assigned to particular groups within that society. To help you understand, consider a society that values individuality and encourages the rule to be proud of personal accomplishments.

In feeling rules, cultural values control the expression of people's emotions. But, this rule also allows people privilege to express emotion to other people of little or no power. An example is where employees of a company tend to be the receiver of negative emotions, like anger and frustrations. People high up in the organization take their anger on employees and get away with it because of their power to control employment.

Another instance where feeling rule applies is where families socialize their children. For instance, children are taught to "feel grateful for gifts" or "not to be angry when toys are taken away". In time, children internalize the rule, controlling what they should or should not feel.

**Emotion work**

This refers to the time and effort you put into how you should feel in specific situations. You become aware of the emotion work each time you experience what is known as the "pinch." The "pinch" happens when you cannot help feeling happy when a person you dislike much is going through a bad day. Emotion work comes into the picture when you make an effort to appear "sad."

## Why people fail to express emotions

Not all people are able to express their emotions. Or they vary in how they express their emotions. While others seem to have no difficulty expressing their emotions, still there are those who experience difficulty in their emotional expressions. There are reasons for their failure:

- Social expectations – Feelings and how they are expressed are shaped by social factors.

- Vulnerability – the fear to give information to others about themselves that would affect how other people would perceive them.

- Protecting others – the fear that what we say or do can upset or hurt others.

- Professional and social roles – the fear that what you express may be inappropriate for your social and professional standing or position.

Often, people who are try to express emotions but burdened with fears and insecurities become ineffective in communication. They tend to:

- Speak in generalities – You often hear them say "I am happy" or "I am sad" Emotional expressions that do not exactly tell you their true inner state. They are ineffective because the statements are abstract and general and do not clearly communicate what it is exactly the speaker feels.

- not own up to feelings – This is expressed when you try to disown personal responsibility for your feelings. Like when you say "you make me angry" which shifts responsibility to the other person. Compare this to the statement which says "I feel angry when you promised to call and you don't". The last statement owns responsibility for the feeling of anger and clearly communicates the feeling.

- Use false emotional language – when you express an emotion but does not really describe what you are feeling. Like, when you say "leave me alone!" You are conveying an emotion, but do not tell what you are feeling. Such statement is false and unproductive. The statement does not tell the other person that it is the behavior you see in the other that is causing what you feel.

# CHAPTER 4

# HOW TO MASTER YOUR EMOTION AND IMPROVE YOUR EQ

Our emotions are crucial to our capacity to confront the challenges we encounter in our daily lives. Notice that when you are happy, you can simply brush aside a task you dislike. Or, how when you are miserable, you view an entertaining activity with gloom or gets bored with it.

Are you aware that the emotions you display at any given time can impact on your relationship with others? For instance, if you chuckle at a friend's tragic story, you appear rude or insensitive. Or, a frown at a friend's joke will be regarded as offensive.

Our emotional experiences influence and shape the decisions and actions we make in our daily lives. While it is true that at a certain level emotions are automatic, they can be controlled and prevented by being aware of our emotions. We need not become servants of our emotions but we can master them and become "architects" of our emotional experiences.

## The reasons behind the limiting emotions

Before jumping to how we can master our emotions, let us take a look at the limiting emotions that you may encounter in day-to-day living. Knowing these negative emotions makes you appreciate the positive ones. And, by going into the negative emotions, you might realize the reasons behind the experience.

## Anger

You feel anger when you fail to get what you want. You react with anger in trying to force things to conform to your way. Anger gives you the illusion that you can control the situation.

In a conflict situation, anger may give you the advantage or perhaps protect your right. When angry, you are trying to tell the other to back off or concede in an argument.

When you are angry at yourself, you are forcing yourself to get things done.

## Annoyance

This is a lighter form of anger which occurs when a person's behavior irritates you or annoys you. What this emotion means is that a person you are interacting with is not behaving the way you want to and you are unable to change it.

Anger and annoyance is the result of things going wrong and your inability to control the situation.

**Sadness**

This emotion signals dissatisfaction with yourself and your achievements. For instance, you feel like something is missing from your life and if only you had a different relationship, job, and house. Feeling this emotion prevents you from enjoying the good things in life.

Nostalgia or when you recall happy memories which happened in the past is another form of sadness. It may not be considered as a negative emotion, but the similarity lies in the illusion that things could have been better.

Frequent feeling of sadness and nostalgic may be signals for you that you are stuck in the past and need to move on.

**Guilt**

It's considered as self-punishment common among over thinkers and deep people. It can also be viewed as a hidden feeling of being superior. To give you an idea, consider the following statement "I am so much advanced that I feel bad about my mistakes."

Guilt is a destructive emotion and is a signal that something within you need to change. But, to change the behavior, you need to know the source or where guild is coming from.

**Fear and anxiety**

These emotions are common in our present time and are linked to self-preservation. Our early history shows us that fear protect our ancestors by preventing threatening situations.

Though the primary concern of these emotions is to warn you of danger, these create images of unexpected obstacles and unpleasant surprises. It is, therefore, necessary that you find the truth behind these negative emotions if you are to benefit from these negative emotions. When identified, fear and anxiety can boost your creativity to solve problems and motivate you to act appropriately.

**Discouragement and despair**

These emotions usually occur when you made several efforts to achieve something and still fail to bring about the desired results. Discouragement and despair also gives you what you think are valid excuses not to pursue with the task and refrain from making any more attempts. You can also take these emotions as signals which tell you that you are tired and need some time off.

**Apathy**

Apathy can be viewed as a hidden rebellion against something. You see this emotion in people who don't have the ability nor the power to rebel in the open. It is a passive-aggressive expression of disagreement and protest against something.

Another interpretation for this feeling is the shifting of responsibility from yourself to another person. For instance, if you are working with a team and your inaction affects the team, it falls on the other members to act to achieve anything for the team.

**Disappointment and frustration**

These spring from discontent when you are unable to get what you want. It is also possible that this emotion comes as a result when people refuse to do what you want. What these emotions tell you is your inability to accept people as they are and life as it is. The result is you feel that life is unfair with you and people don't come up to your expectations.

# Exercises to improve your emotional intelligence

It may be difficult for a beginner to master emotional intelligence. Emotions are subjective and to confront our emotions and be objective about it is a challenge. The exercises listed below follows the key elements of emotional intelligence.

You need not do all the exercises at once. Pick one and work on it until you are comfortable with it and pick another.

**For Self-awareness**

*Monitor what you are doing* – If you are to regulate emotions, you need to be aware of your emotions. At the end of the day, reflect on the different emotions you felt during the day try to identify the emotion – was it anger, frustration, anxiety, or fear? Ask yourself why it happened, what triggered the emotion, what the effect was to you and the others around you.

You could list the emotions you experienced during the day in a journal. Writing them down can help you focus, analyze the emotion, and know more of yourself.

*Check your values* – This exercise is closely associated to the exercise above. Take time to reflect on your values and beliefs and what these mean to you. Your values and beliefs are what you hold important and influences the actions and decisions you make on a day-to-day basis.

Assess the values and beliefs you hold truthfully and how they have helped you (or not) in the past. Make a list of these values in your journal. You can have two columns; under one column list the helpful values and in the second column negative values.

If you see that there are more values with negative outcome, perhaps you need to do something about them or change them.

**For Self-management**

Take a breather – When you are stressed or anxious, you breathing tends to be fast and short. You may not even be aware of how fast you are breathing, and of the effects this breathing has on your heart.

This kind of rapid breathing is called chest breathing which upsets the carbon dioxide and oxygen levels in your body. When this happens, you will feel dizzy, your heart rate increases, and feel other physical sensations like fatigue.

The abdominal breathing is what you use when you are in a relaxed mode. So, when you feel stressed, perform this relaxation exercise which you can do sitting, lying down, or standing:

- Relax your shoulders and take a deep and slow breath through your nose. Hold this for a few seconds. You will notice your abdomen expand and the chest to rise a little.

- Release the air through your mouth slowly. When releasing air, open your mouth slightly and relax the jaw. You will hear a whooshing sound as you release the air.

- Repeat the exercise several times.

*Set aside a time to reflect, reframe, and solve problems* – We often get so absorbed in a problem or a negative outcome of an interaction that we get carried away with our emotions. When emotions go awry, our view of the problem gets distorted.

Set aside a time in the day where you can be alone and reflect on the problem. Try to reframe the problem by asking yourself – In what other circumstance can this problem become positive? Is there a positive side to the problem?

Think about the problem and break it down as to its cause, the trigger, the reaction, and the outcome. Come up with alternative approaches and solutions to the problem and think of possible outcome. Choose the best approach to the problem.

Write down the problem and describe the context. Writing down the problem and its alternative solutions will give you a better picture of the problem and help you come up with the appropriate solution.

**For social awareness**

*Live in the moment* - we fail to live in the moment because our thoughts are flighty – we go from one thought to another with such speed that we forget the present and ignore the person in front of us. We get out of focus and lost in a conversation.

Forgetting the moment can destroy relationships and your chances of social success that you are aiming for. To live for the moment, practice the following exercises:

- Stop thinking about yourself. Loosen up and focus on what is going on in the moment and not on what is going on in your mind.

- Practice to savor the moment. Forget what lies ahead in the future and appreciate the present.

- Pay attention to your breathing.

- Lose track of the time. Constant time checking can distract you from the flow and the moment.

- Develop the ability of acceptance, which means moving towards the problem instead of running away from or ignoring the problem.

- Develop your engagement with the moment by noticing new things, the environment, and the people around you.

**For relationship management**

The little things matter – We often take for granted the little things, and often, we are not aware that they matter to other people. Little things, like saying "Thank you" when receiving something or when someone does something for you. Saying "I'm sorry" when you have offended someone, or the word "Please." Simple words and phrases which go far in building social relationships.

Think of the times you failed to say "thank you" or "please" or how often you omit saying these words. Be conscious of your actions and the next time you experience the same things, remember to say the magic words.

Show when you care – A sure way to mar a relationship is to take the other person for granted. When you someone does a great work, show your appreciation and caring though gestures that express your gratitude and feelings.

Tackle tough conversations – When we are deep in a tough conversation, try to do the following:

- Find out what the shared ground is

- Let the other person speak without interruptions from you

- Listen to the other person's side and try to see and understand what the person is trying to say

- Present your side clearly for the purpose of letting the other person understand you

- Steer the conversation back to the common ground, incorporating what you have learned from the interaction

# CHAPTER 5

# THE ROLE OF EQ IN EFFECTIVE LEADERSHIP

When we talk of leadership, what readily comes to mind is a picture of a workplace. The concept of leadership is broader than that. Leadership manifests itself in schools, organizations, groups, politics, and in families. In a situation where there is no leader, one usually emerges and leads the group.

Makes you wonder what the emergent leader has that makes the group accept the person's leadership.

## The basis of effective leadership

Everyone would agree that the leader is one who can take initiative, has a vision, plan, and strategize. These are qualities that make a leader effective. But, are these qualities enough for a leader to lead a group or a team towards the achievement of a goal?

Working with a group is full of dynamics that influence the direction and strength of the relationship within a group. If things go well, the group becomes excited, enthusiastic, and anticipatory. If things don't go well, members will feel disappointed, frustrated, worried, and angry.

According to Daniel Goleman, it is not what the leader does but how the leader leads that accounts for success. The leader may be very high in intelligence, but the lack or the absence of emotional intelligence in the leadership equation will doom the leader's efforts to failure.

The driving force behind a leader's effectiveness and success is the understanding and management of the members' emotions.

## What happens when emotions of group members are not understood?

You will better appreciate the important role of emotional intelligence in leadership if we look into group outcomes when leadership is low in EQ:

- Work that the entire team needs to do pile up

- Team members perform in different levels (or not synced) and would require different leadership styles

- Emotions are high in social interactions, which makes working with the team difficult

- Relationship in the group is dominated by challenge and is task-oriented instead of mutual respect, cooperation, friendship, and finding a common ground

- Each member seeks power which tends to mute empathy. The more power a member has, the less they feel the need to listen to others.

- Members find no interest in listening and in inquiring. But, for teamwork to be productive there should be frequent and longer discussions with more depth.

- Leaders who are not knowledgeable in facilitating should learn and work on this skill.

- Hard conversations are dodged. This is a disadvantage as emotions can build up until they explode.

-

## Traits of an effective leader

Leaders who possess these traits are more likely to succeed as a leader:

- They motivate and inspire people

- The emphasis is on collaboration among members leading towards synergy and richer experience for members

- They "walk the talk", act with integrity, and are honest with each member

- Work on the foundation of trust, which a leader achieves by consistently acting with integrity and honesty

- They support, motivate, and develop members. They consistently celebrate the achievements of members and move them to learn more and enhance skills

- They build and fortify relationships by communicating to members that each is valued, their concerns important, and will be addressed.

## Emotional Leadership Exercises

Emotional leadership skills can be learned and acquired. Developing your leadership skills need to focus on the interpersonal and intrapersonal skills. Emotional leadership is about the combination of your technical skills, strategic thinking, knowledge, and perhaps more important is the driving force, which is the emotional intelligence.

Here are some exercises you can do to develop your emotional leadership competence. You can write and describe your experiences in a journal. . Writing the experience in a journal gives you the benefit of analyzing the experience better and gives you focus.

1. Recall a time when you were a leader, made a stand, and had others follow you. Ask yourself these following questions:

   - What did you feel?

   - How did the others feel?

2. Recall a time when you made a stand on an issue and later on backed down.

   - What was the feeling like?

   - What were the responses of the others?

3. Recall a time when you were a leader and you did not take a stand on an issue when you should have. Ask yourself:

   - What did you feel?

   - What do you think the others felt?

4. Do the exercises 1 to 3 above, but reverse the position. You are now the employee recalling the experiences of 1 to 3 above and asking the same questions.

If you answer the questions truthfully and objectively, you will locate where your emotional intelligence is, how much more you need to develop, and in which are you have the advantage.

# CHAPTER 6

# 21 POWERFUL STRATEGIES TO IMPROVE YOUR EQ AND SOCIAL SKILLS

It is natural for a person to want to feel wanted and needed; it is vital to a person's self-worth. It is often thought of as the most important set of skills a person can have. Socially competent individuals have the right tools that make them confident in any social situation.

It is also a reality that people view the world through the concept of "us" and "them." It is easy for socially competent individuals to become a member of "us." But, not all are equipped with the tools that would make them socially competent to make them belong to the "us."

Here, we provide you with the tools you need to make you socially competent. Before going on to the skills, we discuss briefly why you need to be sociable.

## Why you need Social Skills

Having a positive social behavior is necessary for our survival. In surviving, society has come up with a set of rules to guide social behavior. Our early ancestors used acceptable social behavior as a survival strategy. To survive, they organized groups which were cohesive in behavior and thinking.

This survival strategy is still true and a reality today. You will find this in your neighborhood and in the workplace. To survive in an environment of people, you need to fit in.

Fitting in within a group means you are trusted, and everything about you is a symbol of belongingness – how you talk, the clothes you wear, mannerisms, and your house. Inability to fit in will isolate you from the group or the crowd and will cause you pain and frustrations.

Social skills are not just about making friends and the desire to belong. It is also about getting through the day, being able to navigate through your day-to-day social situations involving several persons. It involves your ability to make decisions and to foresee the result and consequences of your decisions.

Everything you do in a social context impact on yourself and the other persons you come into contact with. You, therefore, need to consider the effect of your behavior and actions on other people. This is referred to as perspective taking or the ability to perceive what the other is feeling and thinking, or what the motivation is behind the other's behavior.

You can see and understand the behavior of the other person by the tone of the voice, facial expressions, posture, and other verbal or nonverbal cues. And, when you do, you will be able to modify your responses and decide on an appropriate action to achieve your objective.

## Social skills you need and how they help in achieving social success

If there are times that you feel awkward when you are in a group, or find difficulty joining in conversations, you have it in you to change these situations. Social skills can be learned and acquired until they come naturally to you, if you follow and apply the guides below:

*1. Maintain eye contact*

Your eyes mirror your inner self. The same goes true with the other person. Therefore, when you are interacting or conversing with another person, you are receiving, as well as sending information to each other. It is, therefore, a means of communication which is more powerful than words.

Making eye contact could convey several meanings:

- You are telling the other person that you are a good listener and that you are focused and attentive to what the other is trying to convey

- When you make eye contact, you connect with the other person. It could be interpreted as liking the other person and that you are comfortable talking or conversing with the other person.

- On the other hand, not making eye contact could be interpreted as avoidance or that you are trying to hide something. Absence of eye contact could mean a dislike for the other person. Avoiding eye contact has negative effects that will impact on your relationship with the other person.

- Making eye contact is all about trust. Maintaining eye contact with the other person means openness and more likely to elicit trust and respect. You are also telling the other person that you are a confident, self-assured, reliable, and trustworthy person.

*2. Use proper body language*

It is not only your eyes that speak but the whole of your body as well – the way you stand, how you carry yourself, your gestures, and movements. The use of body language can influence or change the interpretation of messages. For example, one way to establish rapport with someone is to subtly mirror their movement.

Depending on how your body language is interpreted, it can either make or break a relationship. It is, therefore, important that you consider the appropriate body language when socially interacting with a person or a group.

*3. Know the difference between being assertive and aggressive*

There are times when you get carried away with the conversation that, without you knowing it, you assert your opinion too much or become aggressive. Such situations might give the impression that the other person is wrong. If you are getting offensive or insulting, you are going into the danger zone of aggressiveness.

*4. Decide on an effective communication channel*

Modern technology has made it easy for us to communicate with other people. But, there are content that are more appropriately conveyed in person.

Email does not contain emotion, neither does the social media. It is difficult to share your feelings and emotions through a computer. Phone calls also are not the same as person-to-person contact.

Know when to say what you feel in person, or if what you need to say can be conveyed clearly through a phone call, or if the social media or email is enough for you to send a message.

*5. Be flexible and cooperative*

You may believe that you are right and that your way is the only way. But, to insist on your own belief may be disastrous in a social situation and will not help you achieve your purpose. Be flexible, open to other possibilities, and cooperative to what other persons may offer. Chances are, there are options you may have missed. Bear in mind that you need people to become successful in life and it will not serve your interest to be antagonistic.

## 6. Accept criticism without being defensive

Avoid getting on the defensive when your ideas or opinion are being criticized. Listen and absorb the criticisms; these are information you could use, especially if coming from an expert.

## 7. Be positive as much as possible

There is a correlation between being positive and success. In addition, people are drawn to others who exhibit this kind of attitude.

## 8. Be respectful towards others

Being respectful, regardless of your position and status in life, is a sign that your regard the other person highly. A socially competent person never displays the attitude of arrogance – that you are more knowledgeable than others or that you are better than the others in the group. You will notice that socially successful people are respectful and humble.

*9. Be true to yourself*

People will sense if you are showing an image of a person totally different from what you actually are. And, when they do, they will come to doubt and mistrust you – something you must avoid if you are building a good relationship. People will accept you if the person you show matches what you say and do.

## Communicating Clearly

There are people who find it easy to communicate their feelings. But, not all are blessed with this ability. There is hope, though, because communicating emotions can be learned. Below are tips that can guide you to become effective in communicating emotions:

*10. Identify your Emotions*

Be attentive to your inner self. We often ignore our feelings, but we can teach ourselves to notice and pay attention to our feelings. You may notice that our feelings are telling us something. When you need to sort out a mix of feelings, identify the primary feeling.

*11. Decide on how to communicate your emotions*

Once you have identified your feeling, think of how you are going to express the emotion. You may want to express your feelings to a particular person. There are times also when it is prudent not to communicate what you feel.

Should you decide to communicate your emotions:

- Assess your current state – For instance, if you are angry, take a few minutes to cleanse your mind and body of the anger

- Decide whom to express your emotion – Expressing your emotion to another person prevents you from imposing your emotion on another who could be hurt

- Wait for the appropriate time to express your feelings – It may not be wise to respond to an emotional interaction when you are stressed, tired, preoccupied, on the defensive, or rushed.

- Choose a setting to discuss your feelings – An appropriate setting may be able to diffuse a negative emotion or boost a positive emotional transaction.

## 12. Own your feelings

If you use "I" in describing your feeling, you have a better chance of making the other person behave the way you want to. And, you will have the attention of the other person who would thoughtfully listen and respond to the expression of your emotions.

## 13. Monitor your self-talk

Learn how to tune in and to monitor your self-talk. Learning this ability can help you manage difficult emotions. When you self-talk, you refer to yourself in third person or by your name. By using this method, you distance yourself from yourself, allowing your brain activity to be less emotionally charged. You can then view the problem calmly and with creativity.

*14. Respond sensitively to the emotions of the other*

Be sensitive to what the other is expressing. Avoid responding in generalities, or attempt to solve the problem, or try to make the feeling go. What a person who is experiencing an emotion needs is to be free to express that emotion to another person.

## Mastering Emotions

As described above, negative emotions have reasons behind their existence in your life. If you experience any or all of these negative emotions, you can still control and master your emotions, following the guides below:

*15. Keep a balanced body.*

You may have heard this advice from many sources. But, a healthy body is essential to a healthy emotional life. Modern lifestyle has you sitting before computers or glued to your desk most of the working day.

You need to move your body to get back into balance. A walk would do as this reduces musings and reduces neural activity which leads to mental well-being. You can also go out and socialize with friends to get you out of ruminations.

There are other ways to keep your body healthy, such as exercise, sleep, massage, time with nature, meditate, social contact, gratitude, and giving.

*16. Distinguish your emotions*

Emotions can mix and blend such that you need to distinguish your emotions and refine it. When you succeed in refining your emotion, you can better regulate it. This is so because a refined emotion gives you the information you need to adjust or change your behavior and deal with the situation.

### 17. Recall positive emotional experiences.

Concepts re reinforced and embedded in your memory each time you focus your attention to them. Cherishing happy experiences and attending to positive concepts will make them prominent in your mind. When needed, these can help you anticipate emotional responses. Consider each experience you make as an investment. It is, therefore, wise for you to construct experiences that you can use in the future.

### 18. Deconstruct and recategorize your emotions

What this means is that you separate your feelings from physical sensations and not let sensations filter your view of the world. For example, you deconstruct your feeling of anxiety to its physical sensation, like your racing pulse. Physical sensations are easier to control than feelings and emotions.

Recategorization benefits you by regulating your emotions. For example in public speaking, when you recategorize your feeling of anxiety as your body's natural response to cope with the situation, you will be surprised to see that you can now face your audience.

Deconstructing and recategorizing emotions have health benefits when you realize that pain is a physical sensation and not a personal catastrophe. To sum it up, your internal state can impact on your emotions and behavior.

The next time you feel a negative emotion, think of it as having a "virus" instead of believing that the unpleasant feeling you are experiencing is personal.

### 19. Identify what you are truly feeling

Be aware of what you are feeling and examine it. Try to separate the logical from illogical basis of the emotion. For example, when you believe that no one likes you ask yourself questions, like "Why do you say that no one likes you?" If you get turned down by one person, does it mean no one likes you?

Look for evidence for your belief. Once you have identified the basis for your belief, you will notice that you are free from maladaptive emotion. Instead of rejection, you feel joy and contentment.

### 20. Cultivate Awe

Unknown to many, experiencing awe holds vast potential for the self and for the whole society. But, our present lifestyle has most people facing the screens that they lose or reduce the opportunities for evoking awe.

Awe is the feeling or in a state of being in the presence of something vast that goes beyond a person's understanding of the world.

It is the experience that gives us goosebumps whenever we see beauty, virtue, ability, threat, and the supernatural. It is what we feel when we see a perfect form and line of an athlete in an Olympic balance beam, see a majestic waterfall, or when we hear roar of the thunder in a storm.

Awe gives flavor to our experience because it encompasses a range of emotions which is similar to elevation, love, admiration, and gratitude. Though, admittedly, awe can also elicit fear, confusion, and dread.

Experiencing awe gives us the benefit of creative and critical thinking faculties, increase in pro-social behaviors (kindness, cooperation, resource-sharing, and self-sacrifice), and improved health.

## 21. Gain new concepts

Stimulate your brain by acquiring new concepts and incorporate them to the old ones. Doing so arms you with the knowledge to predict future behaviors.

For example, when you enlarge your vocabulary improves your emotional health by making you better equipped when confronted with different situations, circumstances, improve your empathy, and enhance your negotiation skills.

You also gain new concepts when you enrich and accumulate experiences by reading books, taking trips, sampling new foods, gaining new perspectives, watching movies, or studying foreign languages. You could even study

# Exercises to develop your social skills

## Practice making eye contact with yourself

This exercise may seem crazy and uncomfortable at first. But, take note that your eyes are the most compelling form of communication. Your eyes can either be intimidating or inviting. So, use it properly. But, before you can use it, you need to practice and master it first.

Face a mirror and look straight to your eyes in the mirror for as long as you can. You may feel uncomfortable and absurd doing this, but resist the temptation to look away. Accept the discomfort – this is part of the exercise.

Once you are comfortable making eye-to-eye contact with yourself at the mirror, smile slowly. Hold this smile. When you start feeling uncomfortable, look away and after a few minutes, reengage.

Perform this exercise until you feel comfortable smiling at yourself.

## Listen to a recording of yourself talking to yourself

Have you noticed that before you talk, you try to filter what you say? Often, we find it difficult to speak up. Try doing this exercise to help you boost your confidence in talking:

Every day for five minutes or more, practice talking out loud to yourself. Just say anything that comes into your mind. The purpose of this exercise is to help you get rid of the filters.

Record yourself when you perform this exercise. The aim is for you to like and trust your voice.

Another way is to take a video of you talking to yourself. When you play it back, you might see mannerisms that you are not aware of. Observing these behaviors in yourself can help you change your habit in talking in talking or conversing.

**Write your stories**

There are people who are adept in telling their stories or in keeping their audience entertained. These people, though, had years of practice telling their stories, or the stories may have been told and retold several times that it comes naturally to them.

You can also become good catching the attention of your audience. But, you need to work on it and apply it in situations. Prepare yourself to become one through the following:

- Think of three or four of your stories

- Pick the one you like most and write it down

- If you are not sure which one to pick, you can test each story with your friends. Observe their response. From the responses you get, you will know which story to choose.

- Hone your story. Too long will make your audience impatient. Your story has to be short and punchy.

- Practice telling your story. You can record or video yourself telling the story. You will then be able to observe yourself talking, and be able to practice your timing and cadence.

**Practice making small talk**

Technology has its downside – one of which is making lose face-to-face contact with people. Conversations channeled through Facebook, emails, text and instant messages made our social skills rusty. One way to go around this weakness is to practice making small talk.

There are people we meet every day – your neighbor, the barista at your favorite watering hole, the workplace, the waiter in the restaurants, and at many more places. They provide opportunities to practice our social skills by having short conversations with them. The purpose is to practice starting conversations.

**Practice confidence**

Many individuals have the misconception that you either have confidence or you don't. They are not aware that confidence is developed and can be acquired through practice. Believe that if you act confident, you become confident. And, here's how:

Go about your everyday business and project confidence. Pay attention to your posture – back straight, head high, shoulders back, chest out, and your arms at your sides.

Walk slowly and with a purpose. Move carefully and deliberately, and when you meet someone, smile and make eye contact.

At the end of the day, recall your feelings. How did it feel the first with your first attempt? The succeeding attempts throughout the day? Did you notice changes in your feelings as you go through the day?

You might have felt nervous at the first attempt. But, you will notice that as you go through the day, you become more at ease with your "confidence" posture.

# **CONCLUSION**

I'd like to thank you and congratulate you for transiting my lines from start to finish.

The mystery of successful leadership was ended with the appearance of the emotional intelligence in the scene. Emotional intelligence is not new, but this has been overshadowed by the predominance of intelligence as the key to success in life and work.

With Daniel Goleman's popularization of Emotional Intelligence through his published works, EQ as a driving force behind life's success to all aspects in life – be it at home, at work, or anywhere else.

Success in life and work is no mystery. Numerous studies on emotional intelligence show that EQ can be learned, developed, and mastered. But, since this quality is internal to a person and, therefore, not easily read nor interpreted, you need to understand and practice the skills.

We have presented in this book the emotional and social skills so you may have a grasp of the concepts. We included simple guides and exercises to help you develop and master the skills need in developing social relationships and be successful.

It does not mean, however, that once you have learned and mastered the skills you stop to learn. Mastering emotional and social skills may require a lifetime of practice. You will be confronted with all sorts of relationships and situations in your day-to-day activities and you need these skills to allow you to face the challenge of the day.

I hope this book was able to help you in your desire to learn about emotional intelligence and how it works.

The next step is to apply the guides and exercises presented in this book. If you do, you might be surprised to see positive changes in you. The days are dynamic and moving, and the best time to start is now.

I wish you the best of luck!

# BONUS CONTENT

# MENTAL TOUGHNESS

# CHAPTER 1

Plato in his "Republic" talks about mental discipline. The Romans believed that men had to study certain subjects in order to become trained in the best traits of life which included basic intelligence, the right attitude towards things as well as core values. The subjects the Romans believed could bring about this type of mental fortitude were music, geometry, grammar, logic, astronomy, rhetoric and arithmetic. In Greco-Roman times these subjects were studied by rote and imitation. This lasted until quite recently and it was only later when pedagogues decided that this type of education was counter-productive and what was required was a "softer" type of education based on moral values and the humanities studies were brought to the fore, however, we will not deal with this and will deal with the basics about mental discipline which in our times is seeing a resurgence in modern thinking.

Today mathematics is seen to be a mental discipline and the idea is to transpose mathematical thinking to common life thinking and problem solving.

One of the ways to achieve mental discipline is to use mindfulness. This is a type of thinking that means we focus on what we are doing right now down to the finest detail. For example; eating. In mindfulness we would focus first on the table. Look at the table, see what its colours are, if it is wood, glass, iron or plastic. How high the table is. What it measures. What is on the table. The cutlery we are going to use to eat, the dishes, the different sets of dishes and cutlery for the other people that will be eating with us. Then we focus on the food. What exactly are we going to be eating. How we will be eating and we focus on our body, our arm reaching for the fork, the hand that grasps the fork, the fingers that hold it, the hand that goes down reaching for the food, the morsel that is placed on the fork. How the fingers, hand, arm and body move as we place the fork in our mouth with the food. The food. Is it hot or cold? Is it crunchy or soft? Does it drip. Is it salty or sweet? The colour of it. The odour of it. We chew it carefully extracting all the nutrition in it. We swallow. We focus all the time on the act of eating and we eat carefully, being and fusing ourselves with the act of nutrition. We are not distracted by other people, tv, a book, the radio, etc. We focus on the act of eating single minded. This is mindfulness and it can be applied to everything we do. By practicing mindfulness every day, we can reinforce our willpower and according to scientists, this can actually increase gravy matter in the brain.

Willpower is strengthened by mindfulness. Willpower is about the refusal to give in, to cave. Willpower is mindfulness in action. By meditating you create a calm space in your mind where your mind is not leaping from one thing to the next and with willpower you force your mind to stay still in the present. This is not easy. You must have tried meditating from time to time and all it did was two things: you got restless and left the meditation room or else you fell asleep. The way to meditate is to use mindfulness to calm your mind and anchor it to the present. Try to sit still and pay attention to what is happening around you or in you at this precise moment. Don´t get distracted. Just sit there and focus on what is happening right now. It is hard. Mental discipline is about doing this every single time you lose focus and this is where willpower comes in. Willpower is what will get you where you want to be every time your attention wanes. The best thing about willpower is that it can be fortified just like your mind because it is like a muscle and you can make it stronger.

Willpower is part of self-discipline. It is the essence of self-discipline. Forcing yourself to do things cannot be done without willpower. Willpower is the grease that the self-discipline machine uses to carry out the motions leading you to a better place inside yourself.

Willpower is what you need to strengthen in order to have mental discipline, it is one of the ingredients you need on your way to a more disciplined mind.

So, we have some things to use now right at the very beginning: mindfulness which is a form of willpower in baby steps. Willpower and these are attitudinal things that we need to use in our quest for mental discipline.

## How do we get mental discipline?

There is no easy way to obtain mental discipline. It takes a lifetime to cultivate the mind. It is almost an art (remember the music, one of the subjects of the Romans that Plato talked about?). There is no way to buy yourself mental discipline. The only way is hard work so prepare for that. Make yourself a plan, a scheme, a way to tackle the issue. Use a notebook to write down all the things you will be doing and keep a sort of mental discipline diary. Read it every day.

Maybe you had a falling out in life, maybe something derailed you from your set path you had. Now while you are in your low moment, or contemplative moment, is the time to set the groundwork for your future which starts now (remember, mindfulness). Now is the time to ditch the old you that wasn't working and get yourself a new you (remember, attitudes). Make yourself abide by a new set of rules. There are ways in which you can use your daily living activities to have more self-discipline. One is getting up early. This doesn't seem like much but if you include it in your new you, it will make you start the day at a different hour and this in itself is going to have an impact on your day. Try it, if you get up at 8 in the morning, try getting up at 7 and see what the world looks like at that time of day. At first you will need almost all your willpower because when you open your eyes and see that it is still very early, your body will be begging you to snuggle down and stay in bed. Don´t. Get up and take a shower. Get yourself a coffee and once you have overcome the temptation to stay in bed and are actually in the kitchen preparing a coffee or a juice, give yourself a pat on the back. It will get easier as your mind adapts to your new schedule and, now that you have gotten up, what about using this extra hour for something special? Try meditation. Go into your living room or your porch with your coffee. If it is summer, sit out there in mindfulness taking in the sensations of the early morning. Stay out there for an hour, it won´t be wasted. Remember, you are rewarding yourself for having gotten up early and you got up early because you are on your way to having greater mental discipline. You are mapping out the steps you need to achieve your long-term goal and don´t forget to keep the forest in mind while focusing on the trees. This is a sample of what a person can do in an easy way to change his or her life.

Mental discipline is something you can learn but it is necessary to practice and repeat it a lot. This is the downside but if you use mindfulness as a tool, you can practice and repeat endlessly and effortlessly after a while because with mindfulness every time you do it is like the first time and this comes with an added thing, a Zen like quality that makes repetition pleasurable. If you practice a sport you will know what this is: it is hitting the ball perfectly every time like in tennis or the runner´s "high", the surge of dopamine in the brain helping you overcome the grind of repetition. If you make it a habit to observe yourself in a detached way while you are doing your practicing and repetition, you will develop your mindfulness and your self-discipline. There are ways that can help you achieve your self-discipline. One thing is to make it easy on yourself, eliminate things that suck your energy, that detract from your goal, for example, if you were dieting, eliminate the snacks and junk food. This is just common sense. It is not a good idea to go to the supermarket at lunch time. Use your common sense and eliminate the temptations that are going to undermine your self-discipline. If you get up in the morning early, do it. Get up and get away from the bed. Move. Go to the kitchen. Do something so you don´t crawl back into bed.

While considering snacks and junk food, remember to focus on healthy eating. This is part of the Spartan like training you will need to foster your mental-discipline so take it to another level and include proper eating in your routine.

Another element in getting mental discipline is to give yourself prizes for achieving things. Don´t make your quest for mental discipline a Marine training site because you will make things so difficult, so almost impossible to achieve that you will fail. Set yourself easy to achieve goals, gradually make them a little harder and set yourself up to win. This is a difficult thing. Lots of people who have decided to embark on achieving mental discipline to immure them from failure and disappointment do so because they have suffered a lot from failure and disappointment. One of the things to watch out for is the paradoxical thing which is: I fasted for one day and didn't eat anything. I am great. Then, immediately after, I rush out to McDonalds and have a binge... Why is this? This is because my mental discipline is so green and raw that I cannot withstand success and need to fail. Then we feel miserable and get all despondent and start considering Spartan discipline... this is wrong. The thing to do is to take it in stride.

Make room for failure and remember to immediately get up and start again or rather, continue. This is the key word: continue. The first time you have a major fail, you will throw this book out the window and go to bed feeling miserable because you failed. But if you go out and find this book and dust it off and read it again, the next time you fail will not be as bad. And this is the wonderful thing. Failing starts fading. Winning starts pushing failing to a side and one day during your mindfulness you will notice how you have changed.

Change: This is the secret to staying young forever. Change. The way in which you no longer do the things you used to do and now do new things or different ones. These are things to consider. If you let yourself change. If you are flexible and use your failings to change yourself, you will find ways in which your mental discipline will start having an effect on what you do every day. Experience is mindfulness in action. Mindfulness is mental discipline in action.

When you fail, which you will do, be sure to take note. Be disappointed, frustrated and angry but don´t forget the forest while you bash your head against the tree. Keep the forest in mind and go back. Get up early and dedicate some early morning silence to mindfulness and pick up where you left off. Practice makes perfect and remember, the Greco-Romans prided themselves on rote learning. So you should too.

Made in the USA
Coppell, TX
04 August 2021